Come With Me,

Love

Song of Solomon for Couples
A 21 Day Journey

Renair Amin

To Lily,

Thank you for taking me with

you...

Glover Lane Press
Publishers Since January 2000
www.gloverlanepress.webs.com

Come With Me, Love Song of Solomon for Couples A 21 Day Journey by Renair Amin

Copyright 2014 by Renair Amin

Edited by Susan Webley-Cox

Cover Design by Azaan Kamau

ISBN-13: 978-0615968162
ISBN-10: 0615968163

The Mission of Glover Lane Press is to Uplift, Empower, Elevate the Masses and Provide American Jobs. Every book published by Glover Lane Press and its many imprints, is printed and manufactured in the United States of America, ensuring and maintaining American employment.

Table of Contents

Preface

Set me as a seal upon your heart,
as a seal upon your arm;
for love is strong as death,
passion fierce as the grave.
Its flashes are flashes of fire,
a raging flame.
(8:6)

Hey, Love!

While a friend and I were in
conversation recently, we stumbled on
the topic of how intimacy in a
relationship can shift over time. This
moved into a deeper discussion which
centered on the ways couples can
bounce back from a place of routine,
disappointment and hurt. I did not
find it coincidence that I was already
working on this book when our talk

took place - it was something long held in my own thoughts.

Depending on the type of relationship, what can influence it in a negative way differs. For instance, in same gender loving unions, factors like internalized homophobia, spiritual (church) rejection, family isolation, hormonal influxes and the general stresses of life itself can wreak havoc. If children are involved, couples can struggle to maintain a sense of intimacy as children take over their time and privacy. A household consisting of only two professionals may find a "deathbed" scenario taking place if work and financial stress impede on their harmony. Regardless of the structure, every relationship is at risk.

Observe the following scenario: A and B have been together for some time.

They have an argument which ends without resolve or compromise for either party. Over time, the unchecked emotions from the argument open the door for jealousy, bitterness, and resentment to enter. One party stops talking and the other stops listening. Soon the only sound that is heard is time ticking away. They become more roommates than lovers. Over time, regret sets in followed by the feeling that there is nothing that can be done to fix it. Or is there?

One of the things that can help couples when distance begins to loom is spiritual intimacy. When a couple has a foundation that is beyond them, it allows them to shift into a different kind of healing. The cracks that form are able to be sealed by a different kind of cement – God. Unfortunately, people have removed God so far out of intimacy (especially their sexual existence) that it leaves them relying solely on human faculties to secure a successful relationship.

Although there are no guarantees in life, every relationship is worth the effort to see if the time spent together warrants going the extra mile. Too often, couples break up without getting counseling, therapy, or even spiritual support. Even if the relationship has to end, it can still be from a place of love and respect for the time that was shared.

What can be done if a couple needs to work on fixing or reigniting the spark in their relationship? This question led me to spend some time in the Song of Solomon, which is one of the most spiritually erotic writings that I have ever had the pleasure of reading. Song of Solomon consists of eight chapters which tell the story of two lovers celebrating the beauty of their love. It is reminiscent of the Harlequin Romance novels that used to distract me during my teenage years, except this story is in the Bible.

Upon first reading it, I was awestruck at how passionately enthralled and connected these lovers seemed to be. I immediately felt in my spirit that there was something here that needed to be shared with other couples looking to establish or rebuild a connection.

I have combined the Holokleria Coaching Method™ which focuses on love and faith and topical scriptures, along with the spiritual guidance I received, to prepare this Journey for you. It is my prayer that by following this devotional using the Song of

Solomon as a guide, you and your Love will find new ways of loving one another. At best, you will have fun going through the exercises and your daily trips into the "garden." At better, by going the "Extra Mile," you and your Love will be able to write your own version of Song of Solomon to be read over and over again.

Renair

Commitment Pledge

This is to be read by you and your Love. After reading what the next 21-days will entail, verbally profess the following pledge and then initial the bottom to confirm your commitment to this Journey:

I, _____, commit 100% to this 21-day process.

I promise to give my all during each activity.

I promise to complete every Journey and in the Garden Experience.

I understand that <u>neither</u> of us can progress to the next day until both of us have done as requested.

I understand that the purpose of this is to bring us closer in communication and intimacy; therefore I participate in all decisions and preparations.

Finally, in order to further guide us along this Journey, I will commit to praying with my Love at least once a day.

Initials:

Recommendations

- Read each Journey in the morning so that you have the entire day to do the activity. Schedule your garden time to make sure you both are able to complete the exercises.

- Maintain individual journals to record your personal thoughts about this experience.

- Try not to judge the experiences. Just enjoy them by being present with your Love.

- If possible, do not participate in any sexual activity during this 21-

day journey. While the activities can serve to be connecting in a way that "inspires" that type of intimacy, it is important to avoid shifting the focus of the NOW of the experience to sex.

Day 1 : Touch Me

O that his left hand were under my
head, and that his right hand embraced
me!
(8:3)

Touching is easy, yet it can be one of
the hardest things for a couple to do in
their relationship. There are various
reasons for this. One could be that
either of you are still bound to an
unpleasant previous life experience. Or,
if you have been together for a long,
time, it can become so routine that it
loses its effect. Either of these can cause
touching to become more intrusive
than enhancing. We have to be
intentional in recognizing the emotion
that comes when we are touched by our
Love. Today's scripture ends with an
exclamation point, which expresses the

sentiment of the speaker. When was the last time you felt excitement by the touch of your Love's Hand?

Let RENEWAL be today's prayer.

TODAY'S JOURNEY: Share a touch whenever you connect with your Love today. Hold hands. Stroke their face. Rest your hand in the small of their back. Put your arm around them. Feel their presence in your life today.

In the Garden...

As you walk in the garden, talk openly about how it felt to touch each other. Sitting face-to-face, take turns answering the following questions:

- How did you feel about the constant touching?

- What was your favorite place to be touched?

- Was there a particular time that a touch was warranted but was not received?

- Did the amount of contact differ from your usual interactions? How?

- How did it feel to be the person doing the touching?

- Based on Today's Journey, would you like more or less touching in your relationship?

GO THE EXTRA MILE: Once your Love tells their favorite place, touch them again.

Day 2: Reflection of Me

Turn away your eyes from me,
for they overwhelm me!
(6:5a)

Spending time with someone is a good thing. However, after a long time, it can shift into a space of familiar, causing you to miss the changes that are happening within the relationship. When was the last time you stopped to really look at your Love? Remember the first time you looked into their eyes and felt an overwhelming emotion wash over you? In that moment you knew that this was going to be the One you took on this Path.

Let REMEMBERANCE be today's prayer.

TODAY'S JOURNEY: Sit face to face, join hands, and stare into each other's eyes for a full minute. There should be no words exchanged or any background noise. Perfect silence. Do not rush the time. A minute in silence does not go quickly. Also, do try not to read into each other's facial expressions. Just BE in the moment.

In the Garden...

Have a seat in the garden with a pen, a piece a paper and an envelope. Take five minutes to write a letter about what it felt like to gaze into the eyes of your Love. Think on the following questions:

- When you stared into your Love's eyes, what emotions arose?

- Was there a feeling that began to surface that surprised you?

- Explain what you saw in the way they looked at you.

After you have written the body of the letter, locate a quote that speaks to the overall experience of today's Journey and place it at the bottom. Seal it in an envelope and put it away. Do not lose it as you will need it later.

GO THE EXTRA MILE: Look your Love in the eyes and then kiss them softly on the lips.

Day 3: Feed Me

Sustain me with raisins,
refresh me with apples;
for I am faint with love.
(2:5)

There is something sensual about food
and something equally as mesmerizing
about feeding your Love their favorite
fruit. It is in this manner that we
become responsible for the
replenishment of not just their mind
but their body and soul. When we
understand how fulfilling it is to pour
back into the One who has been
pouring into us, a new confidence in
our relationship develops. The care you
take in preserving your Love will
eventually begin to spread into other
areas of your walk together.

Let RESTORATION be today's prayer.

TODAY'S JOURNEY: Gather your Love's favorite fruit and prepare them for feeding. You can make this a part of dinner or plan a late night snack but you have to feed one another. No utensils, skewers, or toothpicks are allowed. Gaze into each other's eyes. Enjoy loving conversation. Don't let anything spill...unless it is on purpose.

In the Garden...

As you enter the garden tonight, if possible, pack away any leftovers to take for lunch the next day. This will allow for the memory of your previous night to live on as you reminisce over the experience of being fed by your Love. No one will be the wiser as you smile at the thought of the finger-lickin' good time.

If there are no leftovers, don't worry! You still can relive the moment. During your lunch time tomorrow, take a moment to daydream about how it felt to eat from the hand of your Love.

Afterwards, send them a text or email with one word describing how you felt about the night before.

GO THE EXTRA MILE: Take a picture during today's Journey and save it as a memento.

Day 4: Message Me

Upon my bed at night
I sought him whom my soul loves;
I sought him, but found him not;
I called him, but he gave no answer
(3:1)

Today's technology is beneficial, but it can also be a great hindrance in relationships. Couples often complain that their personal time has been invaded by gadgets. However, if one desires, a hurt can be turned into a healing. When was the last time you dialed your voicemail excitedly, waiting for your messages to begin playing? Hearing the voice of your Love can help jolt you out of a crazy day. Even in distance, the rhythm of their words has the ability to take you right to them. Seek no more...

Let CONNECTIVITY be today's prayer.

TODAY'S JOURNEY: Leave a romantic voicemail for your Love. Try to find a quiet place so that your Love can hear you clearly. During your message, tell them one thing about the day you met that you may not have told them before or share with them a memory that still warms your heart to this day.

In the Garden...

Before you enter the garden, take a moment to listen to the voicemail again. As the words permeate your spirit, think on the following questions:

- How did it feel to receive the voicemail?
- Where were you when you first listened to it?
- Were you surprised at anything that was said?

Think about the voicemail that you left for your Love:

- Was it easy or difficult to leave a romantic voicemail for your Love?
- Was there something you wanted to say but struggled with?

- Is there anything you said that you wish you had not?

When you meet in the garden, do not speak directly about the experience of leaving the voicemail. Instead, focus on how it made you feel to hear such a loving message. Talk about how it affected your day.

GO THE EXTRA MILE: Respond to your voicemail by leaving your Love a message when they least expect it during this 21-day Journey.

Day 5: Beautiful Me

Ah, you are beautiful, my love;
ah, you are beautiful;
(1:15a)

Beauty is a relative trait that is recognized and appreciated by the beholder. One cannot dispute what another deems to be beautiful; they can only appreciate their findings. In relationships, each partner may experience beauty in a way that has superseded its intended definition into simply "amazing." When we focus on what we find amazing about our Love, the things which cause us to struggle become less prominent. It is then and only then, that we can move into a place of true unconditional love.

Let UNCONDITIONAL LOVE be today's prayer.

TODAY'S JOURNEY: Write a list of twenty attributes you find amazing about your Love. Try to think outside of the box. Let your mind wander into all of the things they have done to bless your life. Make sure you check the garden; you will need tools for your visit.

In the Garden...

Bring your list, along with an index card and a pen, with you into the garden. Greet each other with a hug and whisper into each other's ear, "I love you just because..." Upon moving into your conversation about today's Journey, exchange your lists with each other.

Once you receive your Love's list, read it. On the index card, write the three things that stood out to you the most. Create a title/header (i.e. Reasons, I AM, Love is, etc.) Put your card to the side. Take turns slowly reading aloud the 20 things that your Love has written. Then discuss the following question:

What surprised you about the list?

After each of you takes turns answering the question, leave the garden with your index card. Put it in a place where you will be able to see or access it for the remainder of the Journey (i.e., display it on your desk or place it in your wallet).

GO THE EXTRA MILE: Make more than one copy of the index card and display it in various places.

Day 6: Flawless Me

You are altogether beautiful, my love;
there is no flaw in you.
(4:7)

A dear friend once said, "In the beginning of a relationship, there are no flaws. There are just things that irritate us." This is true. Unfortunately, those little pricks of irritation can become thorns, and those thorns can cause us to miss the beauty of our Love. What a pity!

There are times when the thing used to irritate us about our partner shifts into something that encourages us. For example, if your Love is cautious about spending, that may encourage you to save more. If they are adamant about cleaning, that may motivate you to become more organized. These types of mental transitions occur without warning. One day you just look up and realize that your Love is rubbing off on you...and it feels good.

Let UNDERSTANDING be today's prayer.

TODAY'S JOURNEY: Write down something that irritated you about your Love when you first started this path together that has now become a motivating, encouraging, or inspiring factor in your life.

In the Garden...

This garden experience is a little different from the others. You will enter the garden alone. Pull out your paper and read what you wrote. Think on how the thing that once irritated you now blesses you. Ascertain if there are other irritants. Place them mentally in a place of understanding and love. No one is perfect, yet the journey can still be perfect for the both of you.

Take a moment to jot down anything else that may come up. It does not matter if you have run out of room. Write over top of what you already written. Begin to pray for compassion and understanding. Pray for forgiveness for anything you may have been harboring in your heart. As you say "Amen," tear up your paper into tiny pieces and discard. Do this only when you have released any further attachment to the feelings of the things you had written down.

Next, retrieve the envelope from the *Reflection of Me* Journey and give it to your partner.

GO THE EXTRA MILE: Write down one thing that YOU do to irritate your Love. Follow the same instructions for prayer and release. Then, let go.

Day 7: Speak to Me

Tell me, you whom my soul loves,
where you pasture your flock,
where you make it lie down at noon;
(1:7a)

Communication is one of the core elements of any relationship. When couples can no longer talk to one another, it is just a matter of time before there is nothing left to say. Fortunately, there is a way to improve communication between you and your Love. A key to doing this is called Active Listening.

Active listening is often incorrectly defined as "interrupting while one is talking" or "trying to decide your response before the other person is finished." However, it is making a conscious effort to hear the words that are being spoken and to understand the message being sent. The best way to hear what your Love is saying is by actively listening while being attentive, yet quiet.

Let ATTENTIVENESS be today's prayer.

TODAY'S JOURNEY: Sit and listen to your love attentively for ten minutes as they speak of their aspirations and dreams. Listen supportively without input or judgment.

In the Garden...

Sit down in the garden and discuss honestly how it felt to have your Love listen, without judgment or interruption, to you speak about your dreams and aspirations. Do this for no more than twenty minutes, Discuss body language and facial expressions. If there are any uncomfortable feelings, discuss them in a loving manner.

This is a safe zone. Any emotions that come up for you regarding your Love's feelings are to be held for your personal reflection only. This Journey is about listening in a nonjudgmental manner, not leaving your partner with your responsive emotions.

Afterwards, think about the experience and answer the following questions:

- Where you distracted while your Love was talking?
- Did you want to interrupt at any point? If so, why?
- How did you feel about your listening skills?
- What did you learn about yourself? About your Love?

GO THE EXTRA MILE: Practice being an active listener during the remainder of this Journey.

Day 8: Kiss Me

Let him kiss me with the kisses of his mouth!
For your love is better than wine,
(1:2)

According to scientists, your lips are one of the most sensitive parts of your body, surpassing even the receptors in your fingertips! It comes as no surprise considering that a simple kiss can send you swooning for days! Whether the first kiss with your Love was extremely good or terribly bad, you will always remember it. It becomes a part of your story together that lives long into the relationship.

Do you remember the kiss that caused fireworks so passionately powerful it prompted your heart to celebrate? For many couples, such a kiss served as confirmation of their love for each other.

Let PASSION be today's prayer.

TODAY'S JOURNEY: Kiss your Love every time you encounter them. Whether you are waking up, coming home from work, or walking in the room. Kiss their cheek. Forehead. Lips. Nape of their neck. Lips. Wherever.

In the Garden...

As you walk with each other in the garden, talk about how it felt to be kissed repeatedly. Like the *Touch Me* Journey, physical stimulation, if uncommon to the relationship, can feel uncomfortable at first. Sitting face-to-face, take turns answering the following questions:

- How did you feel about the constant kissing?

- What was your favorite place to be kissed?

- Did the amount of contact differ from your usual interactions? How?

- Was there a kiss that was more passionate than the others?

- Based on today's Journey, would you like more or less kissing in your relationship? Implement the change for the remainder of the Journey.

GO THE EXTRA MILE: Add a little flavor. After eating your Love's favorite candy or mint, kiss them.

Day 9: Talk about Me

O you who dwell in the gardens,
my companions are listening for
your voice;
let me hear it.
(8:13)

Do you remember how in the
beginning of your relationship it took
everything in your power to stop
yourself from running to the top of a
mountain and announcing your
happiness to the world? Then, as life
began to take over, the enthusiasm
waned? The good news is that this does
not always mean the thrill in your
relationship is gone. You may have
simply stopped singing about it.

When was the last time you talked with
a friend about your Love? How many

times have you caused eyes to roll, as you went on and on about the blessing that is them? Sometimes, the greatest reminder of how much a person means to you comes as you hear it leave your mouth.

Let EXCITEMENT be Today's prayer.

TODAY'S JOURNEY: Spend time talking about your Love today with a friend. Talk about this 21-day journey and what you desire to see happen. Share your future plans. Just let your Love shine today!

In the Garden...

In the Garden, you will not share today's conversation with your Love. Instead, take at least a half an hour and spend it with them in any manner you desire. Think about what you shared during your earlier conversation and carry it into this experience. If you have children, include them in the garden. Watch a movie, play a game or choose another activity that everyone can enjoy.

The details of today's exercise are not to be discussed at any point during the remainder of the Journey. Just simply evaluate the conversation that you had:

- Is this someone that you can share with again?
- How did they respond?

- How did it feel to talk about your Love to someone else?

Regardless of the outcome of the conversation, remember that its sole purpose was to allow you to share about the blessing of your Love and to bask in the joy of it all.

GO THE EXTRA MILE: Have fun in the garden!

Day 10: Breathe with Me

My beloved is to me a bag of myrrh
that lies between my breasts.
(1:13)

The Word says, "The Spirit has made
me but the breath of the Almighty gives
me life." It is easy to take things for
granted and our relationships are not
immune. Daily living becomes routine.
We begin to expect things to operate as
they always have and for people to be
where they have always been.

A beautiful way to start your day is by
thanking God for all the wonderful
things that you have been given. This
includes your Love. Giving praise for
them shows your understanding that
what you have is a gift. It is inside of

praise that gratitude begins to change the way you view your Love.

Let APPRECIATION be today's prayer.

TODAY'S JOURNEY: Rest on the chest of your Love for ten minutes. Listen as their heart beats and as they breathe. Think on how blessed you are that they have been given the gift of Life. Close your eyes and exist in the moment.

In the Garden...

Write a one page letter to yourself regarding today's Journey. Think about how it felt to listen to your Love's breathing and heartbeat. Write down how their presence in your life has changed it for the better. Include how you feel when they are away from you.

After you complete it, keep the letter in a private place accessible to only you. The purpose of this writing is to be an umbrella on those rainy days. Having something written from a time of peace, love and joy can invoke those same emotions when read at a time of chaos, dislike and sadness.

You do not have to share your letter with your Love unless you choose to. If you do, your Love is under no obligation to disclose theirs. You may want to discuss prior to sharing.

GO THE EXTRA MILE: Write more than two pages.

Day 11: Walk with Me

Come, my beloved,
let us go forth into the fields,
and lodge in the villages;
(7:11)

Sometimes, the world can seem like a never ending merry-go-round. There is always something to do. Our schedules can become so overwhelming that we can barely find the time to catch our breath. With technology adapting to our ever-changing lives, there is not a moment that someone cannot reach us.

It sounds crazy but we live with it, day in and day out. It is imperative that we stop spinning long enough to spend time with our Love. In a day filled with other priorities, this allows them to know that they matter above everything else. It says that even in the noise, we are willing to silence the world to be with them.

Let STILLNESS be Today's prayer.

TODAY'S JOURNEY: Take a walk with your Love. Go to the local park. Enjoy your surroundings. If possible, hold hands. Talk about what is happening in the current atmosphere. Move in the present moment. Make sure you check the garden; you will need tools for your visit.

In the Garden...

This garden experience will be done during the course of the rest of your day and tomorrow. Find a memento that reminds you of the walk you shared today with your Love. Whether it is a poem, picture or even an element of the earth where you walked, i.e. flower, sand, etc., it is imperative that it speaks to the atmosphere you experienced during your time together.

Once you have collected your materials, please package it in a way that it will last a few days and store it for later use. For example, if you collected sand, you may want to put it in a small tube. Do try to complete this task by the next day as it will be needed for an upcoming Garden experience.

If you decide to purchase something, do not make it an expensive gift as it might create an unbalance if your Love chooses not to do so. When choosing to do a store purchase, discuss it beforehand with your Love. If they decline, do not go against their wishes. Also, do not share with your Love what you collected.

GO THE EXTRA MILE: Collect something for yourself that will remind you of today's Journey.

Day 12: Hold Me

Scarcely had I passed them,
when I found him whom my soul
loves.
I held him, and would not let him go
(3:4a)

Have you ever had a day when the only
thing that could relieve your pain was a
hug from your Love? You felt so safe
and cut off from the anxieties of the
world. Your breathing became tuned
with theirs and your heartbeats fell in
sync. There was no place you would
have rather been other than in their
arms.

Hugging is the universal action for
public affection. However, when it is
within the arms of your Love, there is
nothing general about it. The desire to

stay in that embrace overtakes you and time stands still. Like the writer in today's scripture, you do not want to let go. Ever.

Let PROTECTION be Today's prayer.

TODAY'S JOURNEY: Embrace your Love for one full minute. Relax in their arms. Think about how your Love holds you up every day. Receive how good it feels to be encased within their being. Hold on tight until it pains you to let them go.

In the Garden...

This Garden experience involves you and your Love enjoying a movie, television show, etc., while cuddling. You may prefer to listen to music or hold each other in in silence; it is up to the both of you.

During this time, any conversation must be relative to the journey at hand. Stay in the present moment. Do not allow any distractions to infiltrate your time together. Before you begin, agree to how much time you will dedicate to today's Garden experience as there cannot be any cell phone, email, or other interruptions.

Once the agreed upon time has expired, understand that no one is under obligation to extend it.

GO THE EXTRA MILE: Dedicate your entire evening to your Love.

Day 13: Create with Me

We will make you ornaments of gold,
studded with silver.
(1:11)

When one uses their hands to create an expression of love, there is an energy born that resides inside of that gift forever. There is nothing wrong with purchasing an item to say "I love you," however, the saying "it is the thought that counts" is further exhibited by fashioning something from the heart.

As children we relished every drawing, writing, picture etc. that we created. Our excitement grew especially if we were doing it to give to someone else (think macaroni picture frames). As we aged, the time - and for some the willingness - to create, diminished.

Fortunately, our Love can serve as inspiration to create again.

Let CREATIVITY be today's prayer.

TODAY'S JOURNEY: Create something. Whether it is a handwritten poem or a picture of you and your Love in an old frame, make a keepsake that celebrates the journey you are taking together. Make sure you check the garden; you will need tools for your visit.

In the Garden...

This garden experience will be done alone. If you and your Love share the same home, find separate areas to do your work. There are a few rules to understand about this task:

1. You are not obligated to put a time limit in place, however, it may serve to be helpful if one measures the significance of the gift by length of time spent on creating it.

2. This is an expression of love; all judgments should be cast aside if the desire to compare arises.

3. This is meant to be fun! Be easy on yourself! Think more about the purpose behind the gift than overly criticizing your efforts.

4. Do not seek to know what your Love is doing as it may create a subliminal level of competition.

Store the gift for a later journey.

GO THE EXTRA MILE: If applicable, involve the children.

Day 14: Observe Me

What is your beloved more than
another beloved,
that you thus adjure us?
(5:9b)

As relationships grow, couples develop
their own secret language. Have you
ever been in a room with your Love
and held an entire conversation
without saying a word? You could be
on opposite sides of a room but
connect in a way that speaks volumes.

There may be a certain look, gesture or
tone that your Love does that speaks
louder than the action performed. No
matter what is happening at that time,
as soon as it is done, you know
immediately what is being said and just
how to respond to it.

Let DISCERNMENT be today's prayer.

TODAY'S JOURNEY: Think on the
one thing that your Love does or says
that commands your soul to respond.
Is it the way they say your name? Is it
the stern look they give you in the heat
of the moment? What is it about your
Love that makes you melt?

In the Garden...

Spend time talking about your experiences with the journey so far. Assess what has worked, what hasn't and what you would like to keep doing.

Remember this journey is to help improve the way you communicate with each other. If you find yourselves disagreeing on what you would like to remove, implement or increase, <u>compromise</u>. Both of you should leave the garden looking forward to the final week. Kudos to you and your Love on your commitment to this journey!

As you move into the last week, you will find more of an emphasis around dating and having fun. As a matter of fact, let's start tonight!

GO THE EXTRA MILE: Celebrate!

Day 15: Picnic with me

The mandrakes give forth fragrance,
and over our doors are all choice
fruits,
new as well as old,
which I have laid up for you, O my
beloved.
(7:13)

According to various surveys, one of the most romantic dates to share with a Love is a picnic. Having the opportunity to sit down in an informal way takes the pressure off of preparing for a formal date.

Spending time together without worrying about the intricacies of a formal dinner allows for a more relaxing and intimate experience.

Let RELAXATION be today's prayer.

TODAY'S JOURNEY: Have a picnic. Whether indoors or outdoors, schedule a time to enjoy a meal away from the dinner table. Turn your sanctuary into a picnic in the park. Plan the menu together. Make it an "outing" to remember. Make sure you check the garden; you will need tools for your visit.

In the Garden...

Even if you and your Love have to plan it for indoors, let ambiance be your guide. One thing to avoid is adding extra pressure during this experience. The ultimate purpose is to find a way to have a dinner date even if you are not able to afford a formal outing.

This is a perfect time to present your creation from the *Create with Me* Journey. Pick a time during the picnic that you and your Love will exchange gifts. After your exchange, discuss the following:

- What inspired its creation?

- What made you chose the medium/method?

- How did it feel to create for your Love?

GO THE EXTRA MILE: Purchase or create a card to give to your Love. The card's message must be related to the gift you created.

Day 16: Reciprocate Me

My beloved is mine and I am his;
(2:16)

People often say that they desire a
50/50 partnership. The truth is that
most of the time, the percentage shifts.
One is the giver more than the taker.
It is important to remember not to get
caught up in who is giving more. You,
nor your Love, should be keeping a
tally.

If the desire to check the scale comes
into play, recall a moment you received
and were unable to reciprocate. Put
the shoe on the other foot,
remembering how you felt feeling
during that time.

Let RECIPROCITY be today's prayer.

TODAY'S JOURNEY: Pick a random moment to blurt out how special your Love makes you feel. Share with them something they do that makes you feel like you are on top of the world. Do not wait for a response.

In the Garden...

Select a Journey that both of you enjoyed and re-do it. Please remember to compromise. Do not guilt trip or force your Love to participate in a Journey they do not wish to repeat. This should be mutual choice.

You do not have to incorporate the accompanying Garden experience unless you choose to, but it is recommended that you revisit it if there was a journal entry, letter or some other written assignment involved. See if there is any difference between how you feel now as opposed to how you felt then. If you find there has been a shifting, whether positive or negative, in your experience, determine the reason.

GO THE EXTRA MILE: Do two Journeys with your Love instead of one by choosing one each.

Day 17: Rescue Me

The voice of my beloved!
Look, he comes,
leaping upon the mountains,
bounding over the hills.
(2:8)

Do you remember how you felt early in your relationship when your Love called you on the telephone? It did not matter what the topic of discussion was. All you wanted to do was listen to their voice. Even the sound of their breathing intrigued you. Like teenagers, you spent hours on the phone, not caring whether you got enough sleep for the next day.

Let OPENESS be Today's prayer.

TODAY'S JOURNEY: Share a telephone call. Laugh. Talk. Just BE. Even if you are home together, go into separate rooms. If you are unable to do it by phone, you may use a computer to chat. (10-minute minimum. No interruptions)

In the Garden...

Like the Message Me journey, focus on the experience of the conversation. As the words permeate your spirit, think on the following questions:

- How did it feel to converse with your Love in this manner?

- Were you surprised at anything that was said?

Think about the conversation:

- Was it easier or more difficult to open up over the phone or chat as opposed to face-to-face conversation?

- Was there something you wanted to say but struggled with?

- Is there anything you said that you wish you had not?

GO THE EXTRA MILE: Talk with your Love about the conversation. If both of you enjoyed the experience, schedule the opportunity to chat in this manner at least once a month.

Day 18: Inhale Me

Your anointing oils are fragrant,
your name is perfume poured out;
therefore the maidens love you.
(1:3)

It is believed that our sense of smell is connected to our memory. Different scents remind us of places we have been to or of particular moments in our lives. A smell can also invoke a specific response. In 2012 Dunkin Donuts' South Korea campaign saw a 29 percent rise in sales by using "spray radio" which emitted the scent of coffee on buses in the city of Seoul.

Maybe it is the aroma of a meal that reminds you of your first date or the perfume that lingers long after your Love has left the room. You may not even know how to identify the scent. All you know is that whenever you inhale, you are whisked away to the essence of their being.

Let REFLECTION be today's prayer.

TODAY'S JOURNEY: Write down the one scent that reminds you of your Love. It may be the perfume or cologne they wear, an herbal scent or an aroma from their favorite restaurant. Prepare to share it in the Garden.

In the Garden...

Share the scent and the memory that is invoked with your Love. Discuss the following questions:

- What was the best part of the memory?

- What emotions are attached to that memory?

- Are there any other scents that remind you of your Love?

Have your Love close their eyes as you walk them down memory lane. When sharing, try to be descriptive as possible. Take your Love with you as you re-live every aspect of the experience. After you share your story,

let your Love share how they were
feeling during that moment.

Remember to be as attentive to your
Love as you desire them to be to you.
Try not to judge their emotions as they
may have experienced things
differently.

GO THE EXTRA MILE: At some
point over the next seven days, either
wear the discussed scent or recreate the
aroma.

Day 19: Dance with Me

The flowers appear on the earth;
the time of singing has come,
and the voice of the turtledove
is heard in our land.
(2:12)

Whether you are standing eye-to-eye swaying to a slow song or dancing wild and crazy to your favorite tune, the right rhythm can carry you to a place out of this world. Is there a song resting in your spirit that makes the butterflies in your stomach flutter every time you reflect on your Love? Is there a beat that syncs up with your heart every time they come near you?

Besides the essence of the music, there are other reasons to get the feet moving. The chemistry, excitement, and exercise are perfect incentives to take your Love in your arms and dance the night away.

Let HARMONY be today's prayer.

TODAY'S JOURNEY: Share a dance today. Pick your favorite tune and get your groove on. It can be anything you choose as long as you choose it together. This is a time to let the rhythm carry you and your Love to a place where nothing matters but the music.

In the Garden...

Have a dance party. Create a playlist, put in your favorite CD or turn on the radio and get moving! You must dance through at least two songs. Cut loose and let the music be your guide. Use this time to dance away the cares of the day.

At the end of your dance party, you may need to catch your breath, change your clothes, or just fall out! Once you are able to, share how you felt about the experience. Reflect on the following questions:

- Were you afraid to let you and enjoy yourself?
- Did you find it stress relieving?
- Would you want to do it with different music?

- Is there a particular style you would want to try?
- Would you like to do it again?

GO THE EXTRA MILE: Schedule a monthly dance session with your Love. Or if applicable, plan a dance party together with the children.

(Read tomorrow's Journey as you may need to make additional preparations.)

Day 20: Cook with Me

I gather my myrrh with my spice,
I eat my honeycomb with my honey,
I drink my wine with my milk.
(5:1)

Planning a romantic evening out on the town can be so much fun! Getting dressed up makes you feel good and the anticipation of a great time adds to the enthusiasm. Having a "night out, in" can be as equally rewarding. There are ways to paint the town red without ever leaving your home.

How exciting would it be to eat your favorite cuisine prepared by the hands of your Love...and you? Building a five-star night with all of the trimmings is a good way to create a night to remember. Dress up. Play some music.

Light some candles. Make it your night.

Let ROMANCE be today's prayer.

TODAY'S JOURNEY: Prepare a 3-course meal together. Plan the menu. Delegate the tasks and work together to create an appetizer, main course and a dessert that will leave you both begging for more.

In the Garden...

Simply focus on tonight. After all of the work you and your Love have put into this evening, the only thing that needs to be done in the garden is to enjoy the ambiance. Make even the clean-up process one that does not distract from the atmosphere of the evening. It is important to remain in the "now." If you were really out of the house, you would not focus on a ringing house phone, text message, email or any other distraction. Tonight, it is just you and your Love.

If you have leftovers, brown bag it for lunch or put away to eat again the next day. You will have no choice but to feel a rush as you re-live the previous night's festivities through the meal. If you remember, take a picture of the meal and save it as an additional reminder.

GO THE EXTRA MILE: Plan another night out on the town. Only this time, leave the house.

Day 21: Come Go with Me

My beloved speaks and says to me:
"Arise, my love, my fair one,
and come away;
(2:10)

You did it! You and your Love have moved through every *Journey* and *In the Garden* experience! On this last day, there is nothing left to do but celebrate the commitment and work that you and your Love have invested over these last few weeks!

Let today's prayer be RENEWAL.

TODAY'S JOURNEY: Have a dessert and celebrate the completion of this journey! Discuss the experience of the past 21-days. Envision where you will go from here...and then go. Together.

In the Garden...

ENJOY!

Day 22 and beyond...

Prayerfully, you have discovered new revelations and opened the door to new experiences. The work that you and your Love have put into the past 21-days is not only admirable, it shows that you are committed to continuing the Journey from this place. There is a saying: "You can't unknow what you know."

When things show up in your life that seemingly threatens your journey together, reflect on this experience. Go to your prayer closets, seek guidance and then talk it over. Do not let the troubles of the world infiltrate what you know to be true. If you and your Love find yourselves in a dark, go through this book again. Retake the journey. If things seem too far gone, seek counseling, coaching, or assistance from your spiritual leader. Before you let go, do whatever it takes to hold on!

Here are a few things you can do to help strengthen your foundation:

- Continue to pray daily with your Love
- Begin a Bible Reading Plan with your Love
- Find and connect to positive couples/role models
- Fast together
- Meditate together
- Communicate
- Communicate
- Communicate

Did I mention, <u>Communicate</u>?

If all else fails and you still don't know which way to turn, **LOOK UP!**

In closing, I want to leave you with one of my favorite Bible passages:

(I Corinthians 13:4-8)
Love is patient, love is kind. It does not envy, it does not boast, it is not proud. It does not dishonor others, it is not self-seeking, it is not easily angered, it keeps no record of wrongs. Love does not delight in evil but rejoices with the truth. It always protects, always trusts, always hopes, always perseveres.

Love <u>never</u> fails.

"Come With Me, Love"

Feel free to share your experience at
www.facebook.com/cwmljourney

About Renair Amin

Native Philadelphian Renair Amin has turned her tribulations into avenues of encouragement, inspiration and change. A licensed minister, she also uses her educational training as a certified life, relationship and spiritual coach to empower others. A powerful lecturer, motivationalist and author, Renair has published three books - a collection of poetry, Mental Silhouette, self-help book, Pit Crew: How to Survive a Spiritual Pit Stop, and Domestically Cursed: A Story on Partnership Violence. Renair holds an Associates of Science in Business and a Bachelor of Arts in Communications and Culture. She is currently pursuing her Master of Divinity from New York Theological Seminary.

To contact Renair Amin:
Regarding speaking engagements or workshops:
Spyce PR, LLC
spycepr@gmail.com

Regarding Relationship Coaching:
Holokleriacoach@gmail.com

Website:
www.renairamin.com

Facebook:
www.facebook.com/renairamin
www.facebook.com/holokleria1

Twitter:
www.twitter.com/renairamin
www.twitter.com/holokleria

YouTube:
www.youtube.com/holokleria

Other Works by Renair Amin

Mental Silhouette (poetry)

Pit Crew: How to Survive a Spiritual Pit Stop

Domestically Cursed: A Story on Partnership Violence

About Glover Lane Press

Thank you so much for your purchase of this phenomenal book by Renair Amin!

Glover Lane Press is honored to be the publishing house for this unique and one of a kind project!

If you enjoyed reading Come With Me, Love: Song of Solomon for Couples, A 21 Day Journey by Renair Amin, please visit our website for our new, featured and upcoming publications.

Azaan Kamau started Glover Lane Press in the summer of 2000 to give a voice to poets, journalists, and writers worldwide. Azaan and Glover Lane Press have helped countless individuals publish and distribute media in print and in digital formats.

As a woman, one of Azaan's publishing goals is to focus on marginalized or over-looked communities of writers, poets, artist, and photographers. Azaan feels everyone has a story that must be heard or recorded. Another important goal is to use the proceeds from sales of Azaan's books to improve the lives of people around the world. Azaan's companies will feed the hungry, house the homeless, heal the sick, educate and eradicate disease, etc!

Visit us at Gloverlanepress.webs.com

Like Us on Facebook:
Facebook.com/Gloverlanepress

Made in the USA
Coppell, TX
01 May 2022

77304803R00066